The Edge of Greatness—

Your Choices Define You

Written by Chris Davis

CONTENTS

Acknowledgements — 3

Who Am I? — 9

Why Write This Book? — 15

The Purpose — 31

Where Is the Road Map? — 43

Where It All Began — 47

How Many Times Have You Been Fired? — 57

How I Created the Game — 95

Why a Failed Marriage? — 123

Where Is "The Edge of Greatness"? — 131

A Few Tips — 139

Conclusion — 141

ACKNOWLEDGEMENTS

First and foremost, I would like to say to my heavenly father, "I was lost and now found, a sinner saved by grace. I accepted Jesus as my Lord at a young age and I can truly say that no matter what or how you believe, the Power of God is real. It is. Without Him, I would truly fail.

Second, I would like to thank my parents. First my dad, Claude Davis, Jr., for getting my mom pregnant. If he had not lain with my mother, I would not have been the chosen seed. I made it. Beat the odds... I have no clue how many other sperm were in the race, but they failed and then one carrying me made it. And most importantly, I would like to thank my mom, Stephania... you carried me against all odds. I will never forget the story you shared with me about leaving the abortion clinic just as you were about to commit an unthinkable act — taking my life. I have no idea what you felt or thought or looked like, crying as you walked three miles to get back home. But THANK GOD!!! I am still here.

I never knew how much you gave up for me and my five brothers. You provided a roof over our heads, food to eat, and beds to lie in. I can never know how much you sacrificed for your six boys, but I swear if this book makes it to 100,000 copies, I will get you a home and whatever else you like. Mom, I love you more than you know. As a single parent I would never wish the burden of raising six boys alone on anyone, but somehow you pulled it together and all of us graduated from high school. We attended or graduated from college. Three with college degrees, one of us with a master's degree, one semi-retired by 41. And me. You did the best you could with what you had and you made it work! Thank-you!!!

To my boys – Jordan, Jeremiah, Darius, Amir, and Samuel, every day you teach me to be a better dad. I love you. I know it is hard to be a son to a tough dad. But know I am trying to groom you to be better men than I could ever be. My recent transition from single dad to teacher and life coach has been one of great pleasure. I owe you everything because teaching you has made <u>me</u> a better man.

What you do not know is that I share every one of my failures and successes with you so you don't make the same mistakes I did. I pray you take the seeds that I have planted and allow them to be watered so God can give the increase.

To my former wife, Elyse, I put you through hell. Every time I came home and uttered those dreaded words, "I got FIRED," I am sure your heart sank a bit more. But through it all you stayed with me. When I had a bright idea, whether it came to fruition or not, I was able to tell you. I know I am a tough guy to love, but you did. I am eternally grateful for the love you gave. We tried. Married at a young age, we grew in different directions, but the fact that we tried is a testimony in itself. You gave me 4 amazing children and 15 years of ups and downs. You deserve honor and respect.

To the late Bishop Eddie Long… omg!!! What an amazing man you were and what an impact you had on my life. You spoke with such power and as you used to say, profuntatity (not a word, but you made it sound good). You helped me become a man. You spoke into me and allowed God to show you how to create men. You did something Martin Luther King, Jr. could not do. You duplicated yourself by pouring out your life to others that they would be more like Christ. I only pray I can be the man God desires me to be. I know you saw more in me than I did in myself as a young teen. Your legacy will live through others and through me. Thank you more than you know. I did not get to say my last goodbye, but I still bid you adieu!

To my friends, family, relatives, I have had some crazy ideas and yes, I tried to believe they all would come to pass, but they did not. It was worth a shot anyway. Friends often come and go, but mine make me feel wealthy. Knowing who is in your corner and has your back in good and bad times is how I define friendship. Dear friends, you are the reason I feel rich, not the money. The money helps though! ;-)

WHO AM I?

Who am I? By birth I am Christopher Dewayne Davis, born to Stephania and Claude Davis, Jr, at 7:21p.m., 12/31/1979. When I was born, I was rejected by Suzanne (pseudonym), the woman who shared a room in the hospital with my mom.

As the story has been told to me, they both were expecting baby boys.

"What are you going to name your son?" my mom asked Sue.

"I am going to name him Christopher Dewayne," Sue responded.

"Oh, I like that," mom exclaimed. "I think I will do the same!"

Sue replied angrily, "Hrumph. I will not name my son the same as yours!"

"That's fine. I still like it."

"So you are going to just steal my son's name?"

Mom responded, "Steal? Hardly! Look, Sue, you do not own the name and it's something I like."

"Then I am going to name him John Peter," Sue stated defiantly.

… And that's how I got my name. But my name is not the sum total of who I am. I am more than its meaning, Bearer of Christ. I am a human male who loves to create, decide, and exist in happiness and joy. I am a father, husband, brother, friend, foe, son, cousin, uncle, bonus dad, and mentor. I fancy myself an ideation specialist, which means I have an idea for every day of the week. I feel as though I can resolve any problem, even if it is not fixable by me. I also used to be the guy who was good at everything and focused on nothing. Now I am the one who focuses every ounce of energy on my life purpose, which is to create. I was designed to create.

Knowing your purpose and discovering it is an amazing feeling. Ask yourself, "What was I born to do that no one else can do?" On the following pages, write down why you believe you were created. It will help you find your purpose and give you direction when you feel lost.

WHY WRITE THIS BOOK?

Why write this book? What is the purpose of the title, *The Edge of Greatness*? Why the stories? Who decides what is great and what is not great? When does the truth of why I wrote this book reveal itself? Why is all of who I am and where I come from important?

Why write this book?

Honestly, I had no intention of actually writing a book. I never wanted to be an author or tell the stories of my family or my childhood. That is not how I got started. The only writing I did was in my journal and that was about the girls I used to love/like and kiss. Seriously. I aspired to be a lawyer because I was told I'd be good at it. Quite frankly these stories embarrass me to some extent. Some are truly humiliating and others are humbling. When I began writing this book in 2008, I was broke, trying to reinvent myself, searching for ways to achieve success. I had failed so many times that I figured what the hell, I could at least write about it. Maybe that would be the path to realizing my dreams.

But success did not come in the form I thought and I failed more than I care to admit. I just wanted to stop being broke and have something to be proud of. I wanted, needed to stop being/living the life of what I perceived to be a failure.

Another impetus for writing the book was my big sister from church, Kimberly Sharkey, author of *Seasons of Intentional Relationships*. She admired the board game I created, the story of which is central to my book. Knowing that few blacks have ever come up with such an unusual concept, she suggested I write a book enumerating the steps I took to move the game from concept to reality. Kimberly believed there were people who may want to design a game but had no clue how to go about doing so. This would provide them with a blueprint. So I started.

During those years, my wife was working full time and I had lost my job, again. I knew I had a story to tell but never knew how to tell it or even if someone would care enough to read it or listen to it. My self-confidence was through the roof on the exterior, but on the inside I was filled with doubt. To others, it seemed like whatever I undertook was sure to succeed. Most people who knew me from high school or college years will tell you I was self-assured. But those people only knew my outer self, the part of me that I show to everyone, the classic version of me that is most outwardly expressed.

Thanks to the world's greatest therapist, Natolie Warren, creator of *The Whole Woman Experience* and author of two phenomenal books, *Experiences of a Whole Woman* and *Perfect, Complete & Lacking Nothing*, I have learned that we are comprised of four parts. Below I have listed each part and will briefly discuss what I have come to learn about each one.

It is important to understand that I am not a therapist, not licensed to discuss your specific situation, or guide you in your choices. I am sharing my experiences with you, allowing you to glean knowledge of what I know and have come to learn. It is very important at any stage of your life, when presented with information, to take in what is good for you, listen to it all, and decide what you can eventually throw away. I am sharing what I have not thrown away.

Complete Personality Pie

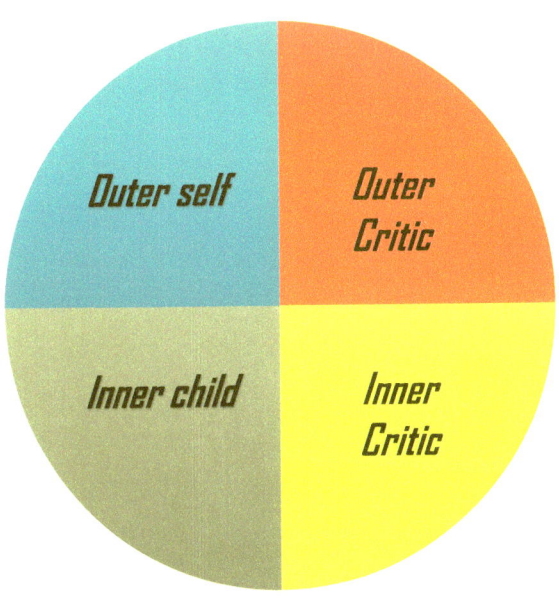

The personality I showed most was my **outer self** (upper left corner). The outer self is the personality that most people already know and see. For me it was the exuberant, sometimes loud, fun-loving, good time character. I was also obnoxious and lazy with my words at times, meaning I would say anything without thought or consideration for others. I did not take care with my words and thus ended up hurting people without knowing that I was toxic and not whole. I only showed a part of me to the world. From the bottom of my heart I apologize if I offended anyone at any time.

I was confident outwardly. I was sure I was the next biggest thing cooking. I was sure because others told me I was. In college I was told, "You are a diamond in the rough." "You are special." "You are the man!" "I can see it; you are destined to be great." Parishioners in my local church claimed I was anointed. "You remind me of this mega pastor or that mega preacher!" All these thoughts filled my head and fed my outer self and ego! I always walked around with an attitude because I knew I was the next great thing coming. I acted like it. I talked like it. But in truth I was nowhere close to being anything great. Hell, let me be downright honest with you. I was a complete failure.

By many standards, I had done nothing good or right. I dropped out of prestigious Morehouse College in 1999. Had a baby without being married in 2000. Had a home foreclosed on in 2006, when I could have done a short sale or used income tax money to save the home. Read books that said it's okay to be a college dropout and not finish your degree because others have done it too and you are just like them. I was not like them. I was me. Different. From 2003-2004, I blew through fifty thousand dollars with NOTHING to show for it except loss. No savings. No paid off debts. No investments. No new ideas that would generate cash to sustain me as job losses piled up. Lastly, I divorced in 2017. All failures in one sense or another. But that was not what others saw. My public persona was that of a confident, proud, accomplished businessman, while the inner me was screaming, desperate to find its place.

The outer self is the personality that most people already know and see.

I was depressed and did not even know it. I was afraid to share my treasured thoughts, believing this would protect my outer self and keep it safe. The **inner critic** is your self-talk, the thoughts you have about yourself that you generally do not share with others. You criticize yourself and your accomplishments. You may even belittle the good things you have done, talking yourself into and out of doing things.

The inner critic is your self-talk, the thoughts you have about yourself that you generally do not share with others.

You criticize yourself and your accomplishments.

The inner self is about what cannot be seen: feelings, intuition, values, beliefs, personality, thoughts, emotions, fantasies, spirituality, desires, and purpose.

The **inner child** is an individual's childlike aspect. It includes what a person learns as a child before puberty. The inner child is often conceived as a semi-independent subpersonality, subordinate to the waking, conscious mind. Most adults are quite unaware of the inner child. And this lack of awareness is the primary cause of so many behavioral, emotional, and relationship difficulties.

But that is not why I wrote the book. The inspiration occurred during an intensive career fair hosted by world-renowned poet Hank Stewart, author of the book *The Answer*. I looked forward to participating in this informative program, which I had attended the previous year. Upon entering the classroom, I spotted a man I recognized from the 2013 seminar. As so often happens in life, this was no coincidence. The first time I met him, he listened to me share my story and said, "Man, you need to put that stuff in a book. People would love to read it!"

What he did not know was that back then I figured I was smart enough to think of writing a book, but in reality I was not smart enough to know how to fill the pages or get it published. He clearly remembered me from the prior workshop, asking if I had written my story and published my book yet.

Ashamed, I replied, "No, I have not."

The truth is, I could have written my story about the experiences of job loss and arrogance, but who wants to read that? Not I! Sure, these are included in my book because job loss and failure are a huge part of my story and where the book originated. But it is not the totality of this narrative. I wrote this story because I believe the words that fill these pages will help heal some wounds and hurts that seemingly damage so many of us.

It is not just a story about overcoming, but that's included. It is not a story about challenges, but that's in here too. It is about mental fortitude, toughness, grit, failure, success, hard work, passion, doubt, fears, loss, hope, learning to reprogram my mind, rejection, discipline, and so much more. Its purpose is to bring clarity to some. Occasionally we need to turn on the high beams in the car to see through the fog. And it is my sincere belief that this book will give you clarity to see through the fog and overcome. Allow you to define or redefine who you are and the direction in which you wish to travel. Remember forward is a great choice of direction! I want to give purpose to those who read the book. Lastly, I wish to give you hope. Because if I can make it, so can you.

I am purposely writing for you, yes you, to show you that it does not matter how long it takes to reach a destination. Just keep going until you get there.

This year as I write, it is a full 10 years later. Ten! I have experienced loss - friends, family, a pastor, spouse, and probably will lose and gain more as my life continues forward. But know this for a fact, you must continue – forward!

"The only way forward is – forward"
    Attorney at Law, Reginald Winfrey, ESQ

30

THE PURPOSE

What is the purpose of the title, *The Edge of Greatness*?

If the title were *The Edge of Mediocrity*, would you have picked it up? I am inwardly smiling with you because clearly the answer is a resounding, "No!" According to Jim Rohn, greatness is achieved by affecting or serving many. It is not defined by the things we acquire over time, but by whom we affect during the time we have on earth.

Martin Luther King, Jr., the greatest civil rights leader of our time, affected an entire generation. Michael Jordan, considered to be the best basketball player ever, changed the sport unalterably. Winner of 6 NBA championships and two three-peats, he had a lasting impact on the way kids today play the game. Wardell S. Curry Jr., arguably one of the greatest basketball shooters of all time, changed the way teams guard players, thus affecting the way children now play basketball. Dolly Parton and Elvis Presley were game changers in the music industry, impacting the lives and careers of many.

But this is not the only key to greatness. MJ, whether Jackson or Jordan, is a rarity. If everyone were like them, they would no longer be special. How then can you personally apply greatness on an everyday basis and not live in the limelight? Can greatness still be achieved? Yes! You can achieve the most remarkable things without being a superstar.

The purpose of the title *The Edge of Greatness* is complex but simple. Complex because it will not be easy to remember to exercise your mind daily and take time to think through your critical decisions. That is never a simple process. But it is simple because anyone can do it. Anyone can achieve it.

The title of my book came from moments in my life when I stood at the corner of decision and opportunity, at the intersection of success and potential failure, trying to decide when or if I would make the right decision. One can contemplate making a decision but scurry away from it because of fear. Not making a decision is still a decision nonetheless. I passionately believe that greatness is service to many and in order to serve the many you must decide which path you will take. The edge of greatness is the series of decisions you make that lead you directly to the path to serve many. Thus the title. You must make a decision that will lead you to the path that will allow you to serve a few, a lot, hundreds, or even thousands.

Consider for a moment Pastor Jamal H. Bryant, Senior Pastor of New Birth Missionary Baptist church in Atlanta, Georgia. He left an A.M.E. church culture and family, which he built from the ground up starting with fewer than 50 members, to join a Missionary Baptist church. Because of this decision, he affected many lives and changed the course of his own life.

Consider Lebron James, number one draft pick in 2003 by the Cleveland Cavaliers. After playing with the team for several years, a championship win still eluded him, so he left for the Miami Heat, winning two out of four championships while there. Then, after leaving the Miami Heat, he returned to the Cavaliers, who had 2 or 3 number one picks in back to back years and now could build a better talent pool of players. In dramatic fashion, he ended up winning an NBA championship in his home state.

Consider yourself. Today. Where are you? What decisions must you make that will change the direction of your life? Are you worried it will not work? What if it does work? Are you wondering if you should return to school? Apply for that job? Start a business? Leave a toxic relationship that is not helping you grow? Should you take that promotion? Move to a new city? Why, I ask, do you hesitate? If you have planned for success, then sometimes you must also plan for things not to work out as well.

Doing so will keep your head out of the clouds, thinking lofty and unrealistic thoughts. I am not suggesting that you take a leap of faith without calculating the risks involved, but I am emphatically saying, "Stop wondering if it will work out and make a decision." You deserve it. Your kids, family, friends, or future depend on, hinge on you making a decision that can alter your life and you should begin the process now.

Take a moment here on the following pages to write down decisions you must make. Leave space between each goal you want to accomplish or decision you must make and then add at minimum 3 to 5 steps to make them happen. Leave room for things you may miss. Ask your close friends for their input and LISTEN. Listening doesn't mean that you have to do exactly what they are saying, but it does mean that you can take what is good for you and leave out things you do not think you need; however, you should remember those things they said just in case you may need to utilize them in future decision-making.

Third, write down dates by which you want to achieve these goals. When writing down your dates, be honest. Be real with yourself and stick to it. If the date comes and the decision or goal is not accomplished, decide if it is still something you wish to do. Understand that a goal without a deadline is just a dream. And nothing, I mean nothing, comes from dreaming but sleep. Ohhhh, here is the most amazing part of setting your deadline. If the day comes and you have not accomplished it yet, reset it. But be honest with yourself. Consider an accountability partner, someone who will keep checking on your progress and getting on your nerves, bugging you to accomplish that which you said you wanted to do.

At the end of the day no one can make you do it other than you. If you choose not to answer the phone, then it is not the fault of your accountability partner that it did not get done. If you choose not to move on the action steps you wrote down, then it is not your friend's fault either. Accountability does NOT require anyone to force you to do something. It is the process of reminding you to do the thing you said you would do long after the feeling and excitement about it has waxed cold.

Hence the title, *The Edge of Greatness*... you must decide on an action plan and ultimately your choices will define you! So get off your ass and get to it. I intentionally inserted blank pages so you can begin to formulate your plan. Blank pages so you can fill them and fulfill your goals. Ready? Set? GO!!!!!!!

Greatness is achieved when you start to believe that you can be better every day. Even if you failed today, you still have tomorrow to begin again.

40

WHERE IS THE ROAD MAP?

Where is the road map? How does one get there? Where do I start? My plan is to share with you the experiences that have led me to this point and why I believe at each moment I have been close to the edge and decided to jump over it.

Where is the road map? I do not have it. When I began, I had no clue of the direction in which to go, so I had to blaze my own trail. This may put you off because many fields already have experts who willingly share for free ways to accomplish anything. Hell, to be honest, you can buy _____ *for Dummies* books, which claim to provide everything you need to accomplish whatever it is you set out to do.

Why the stories? The truth is, it's the stories or events of life that batter us, building our character. But the stories I am sharing are just the beginning. It is the experiences that shape you and make you who you are. It is through those same experiences good/bad/indifferent that you learn and figure out how to choose better or for some not choose at all. We are nothing without those experiences. Nothing without the decisions we have made to get to the place we are currently in.

I am nobody greater than the next person that I deserve to be listened to, published, or spoken of. But do not get me wrong, I am not this sheepish, lowly mule. In fact, I fancy myself to be quite different from that. I am a valuable man, but humbled…humbled by experiences and humiliated by circumstance.

However, according to astrology I am supposed to be among the greats: Lebron James; Martin Luther King, Jr.; Jim Carey; Michelle Obama; Betty White; Denzel Washington; John Legend; and the list goes on.

We all have stories to tell, stories we remember fondly. They inhabit our inner thoughts and feelings and sear themselves into our souls. At times we form a bond with a story such that when it is told we may shed a tear, laugh inwardly, or guffaw loudly. These stories bring smiles when we reminisce about the good times and sorrow when recalling the bad. The truth is… everyone's life is a story. These little daily stories, compiled over time, are relived and passed along. And that is why this book is here… to give you the courage to retell your story, because someone needs to hear it. I pray mine inspires you, blesses you, helps you have a different perspective, and gives you courage. And lastly, I hope you find your Edge of Greatness!

If the stories are the beginning, then the ending is the choices that you make or made to arrive there.

At times we form a bond with a story such that when it is told we may shed a tear, laugh inwardly, or guffaw loudly. These stories bring smiles when we reminisce about the good times and sorrow when recalling the bad. The truth is… everyone's life is a story.

WHERE IT ALL BEGAN

I was born December 31, 1979. I lived in Little Rock, Arkansas for the first 3 years of my life. As a three-year-old child I experienced some of the worst things a boy could ever imagine. Just listen:

Me: "Dad, can I have some of that?"

Dad: "Here"

At 3, my dad gave me a can of beer, which I immediately spit out because it was the nastiest thing I'd ever tasted. Beer. At three!

As a toddler, I watched my drunken father push my mother down a flight of stairs in front of our house. She lay bleeding on a gravel driveway. Although I was too young to speak on these matters and not old enough to know what to do, I will never forget this horrific incident.

Why does that matter? To me it matters because it is part of my life story. It speaks to the shaping and molding I did or did not receive as a child. My father, although I have forgiven him since, was in my opinion a bad father during my formative years. He wasn't a bad parent just because he was abusive, but because I did not learn anything other than how to be physically aggressive. Some good did come of this because without this lesson I would not have learned that I could overcome the anger and be a calm person inward and outward.

Now do not think I am a pushover. Not at all. Every day I work hard to prevent my anger from getting the best of me. I will admit I am not close to being perfect, but I practice self-control daily.

Another indelible memory was a whooping I got over cheese balls. My two older brothers and I ate an entire canister of cheeseballs; however, <u>they</u> had the foresight to wash the evidence off their faces and hands after they finished eating. When my dad came home, I got the beating of a lifetime. Why? Well, because the evidence was all over my face and hands and I was too small to wash it off myself properly.

Not long after this incident, we moved to Buffalo, New York and I enrolled in Montessori school. I remember my grandmother telling me she taught me my ABCs and 123s... Who does not love their granny?

Fast forward a few years. At the age of 7 or 8, I lived upstairs from Ma (in my granny's house). I learned how to cook eggs, but always burned them. I learned how to clean or at least watch my older brother Rees clean the stove. I was the annoying kid back then. I got on Rees's nerves so bad that while cleaning the kitchen he sprayed me directly in the eyes with the oven cleaner. (I stress the importance of not doing this, as it is a dangerous thing. Please do not try this at home).

Shortly thereafter my mom purchased a home at 18 Chester Street. At the time I thought I had a lot, but did not know how poor I was until I became an adult and looked back on the things I experienced. This house had 6 bedrooms and 2 bathrooms. It was basically a two-family house, a whole home upstairs and a completely separate one downstairs. After a few years of living in this home our bathtub stopped working and we had to bathe at Ma's house, a 1/2 mile away, or my Aunt Tina's house, 1/4 mile away. The toilet also stopped working so my brothers and I used a 5-gallon paint bucket as our bathroom. I had epic fights with them over who was responsible for taking it out multiple times each night. It had to be dumped in the sewer across the street, a source of great embarrassment. This was my life for as long as I could remember. Although the house has since been torn down, the memories remain.

I come from a town where the pizza is bar none… and chicken wings were invented. Buffalo! That's right! I grew up living upstairs from my grandmother during the early part of my life. After my oldest brother burned my mother's brand-new carpet, I think my mom said it was time for us to move. I have many fond memories in that home. They are not all great ones, but fond nonetheless.

Like the time I got whooped with an extension cord when I was 11. My oldest brother had scalped our Buffalo Bisons baseball tickets for $5 each. We hopped the NFTA (without paying the fare) to the Amherst train station to play video games at the arcade store on Main Street. Then instead of coming straight home, my brother decided to play basketball behind the high school around the corner from our home. This was pre-cell phone days, pre-pager days, so my mom had no idea where we were. The look in her eyes said it all. She wore us out that night. Those 3 licks with that cord felt like 10,000!

Or the time daddy Joe, my grandfather, tried to whoop me with a belt and since he was much older and his strength had faded, it felt like a 2-year-old was hitting me. Yeah, sure the belt stung because after all it was a belt, but dang (a word my mother strictly forbade us to use). I cried only to make him feel as though he was doing something. I know, I know… shame on me... but I told you I had really fond memories.

Like meeting Chavon, the girl across the street, that my brother (who shall remain nameless...) was crushing on forever. Or the 3 brothers Marcus, Marquis, and Martin, who could never come out and play. Or beating the Muslim brothers in street football every time they came up the block to play. (They were really, really fast). Or snowball fights, jumping on the balcony into the snow, making tunnels in the front yard. Yep...fond, fond memories...

Why is all of who I am and where I come from important? Why the stories? The truth is it is the stories or events of my life that crushed me, strengthened me, and made me who I am today. I am nothing without those experiences. I would just be living. Nothing would happen to set me on a different path, a path to another place.

My journey from high school to college was an important transition in my life. I only applied to one school, Morehouse College, to which I was accepted. But I neglected to inform them I would be attending and just showed up on the first day of classes. Thankfully, I was able to enroll and begin my college education. I finished 1½ years. Then I started working because I had a son on the way and did not have enough money for tuition.

But before I get way ahead of myself, let me take you back to when all this got started…when I was too young to notice a pattern and did not know enough to ask what I was doing wrong.

Why would someone fire a 14-year-old kid? Keep reading and you will find out…

THE MOMENT YOU THINK YOU ARE GOOD, KEEP YOUR EYES OPEN FOR THE NEXT CHALLENGE.

HOW MANY TIMES HAVE YOU BEEN FIRED?

Why fired? Well being fired has been a tragic part of my life since I can remember…

I have no job as of today, 07/18/08. I am broke and the bottom line is I am too afraid of allowing the shadows of failure to swallow me up. I have always thought that money and fame would be mine because so many events have happened to form my ideas of who I am to be. And so many say, "Man, Chris, you are a diamond in the rough." Or, "I can see greatness in you." For the longest time I believed the hype and tried to live up to it. In fact, this quote says it all, "You cannot consistently perform in a manner that is inconsistent with where you are."

For years I was broke. I made a vow that I would always add something of value to my person every time I ran into some major money. But who wants to talk about the "what -if's" and the "I could-haves"? I know I do not. I am flat broke. It is no fun.

Here is my story.

At age 11, I got my first job as a newspaper boy with my own paper route. Actually I was running the route when I was 10, but because of some New York State law I could not have my own route at that age. So, on January 3, 1990, when I turned 11, I began my first route. I delivered papers Sunday through Saturday. On Sundays when I had extra papers, I sold them to a few customers who only wanted to pay for the paper without the subscription. This generated a modest profit, but a profit nonetheless. I also sold Friday and Sunday papers, which had the sales ads, for $2. The Friday paper was $0.35, so I made $0.15 plus the cost of the paper ... but since they were extra, it was truly all profit.

My responsibility was to put the ads in the paper and deliver them before 5:00 p.m. on weekdays and Sunday before 11:00 am church service. I remember braving the $10°$ morning air, snow pelting me, as I faithfully delivered those papers to each of my 50+ customers. Most days I walked to deliver the papers and the pavement was always cold. But I bundled up and did my best to keep warm. Thank goodness I had a great mother to provide me with a coat and scarf and gloves.

I remember one house, 78 Northland Avenue, that I think had mentally disabled folks. I was always afraid of this house because I thought they would somehow try to grab me, pull me into the house, and torture me. Although, I was only 11 at the time, I swore it would happen. I was terrified to drop the paper off… the house was a new house back then and probably one the largest on the route. It was big, brown, and scary and although it was silly, I was terrified.

The best part of the route was getting paid the extra money. $35 a week for delivering these papers was probably enough for the average adolescent, but I spent it so quickly that I was always hungry for more money. The extra money paid for my 3/$1 drinks. I used to wonder why my other paper route friends made more money, but that was probably because I did not collect the payments from the people. I was an entrepreneur back then and still am to this day, but I sure had a lot to learn. I got started by hustling the extra papers my route manager would leave. There were some people who only wanted the $1.50 Sunday paper and I told them I could deliver 3 Sunday papers weekly to them for $5.00.

One cold Sunday morning on the way home from the route, I found myself catching up to my older brother Rees. Both of us were headed back home, having finished our separate paper routes. Walking down Waverly Street to Woodlawn Avenue, we turned towards our house. I was a silly clown back then and like most pre-teens I did stupid things. We noticed our oldest brother, Jeff, coming down the street in the minivan and I said to Rees, "Watch this!" As Jeff approached on the ice-slicked road, I swung my empty paper cart at the van, pretending I was going to hit the car. Then I quickly jerked it back, suddenly finding myself on the ground as the force and weight of the cart brought me down. Once Jeff's car finally stopped, he ran to my side. As I lay there, he instructed me to get up, but I could not feel my foot.

"Wiggle your toes," he suggested.

"I am," I replied.

"Awww, shoot!!" he muttered. If you know him, you know he did not swear back then. A few hours and a hospital visit later, I was home in a foot to waist cast with a broken tibia and fibula on my right leg. Now of course you are thinking, *Damn that was dumb...* Yeah... but I was also 11 with no self-discipline.

Every time I tell that story someone asks, "Your brother ran over your leg?"

And I say, "Yes." I own what happened. I made the decision to swing that cart. He did not choose to or desire to hurt me. And yes, it's perfectly fine to laugh... everyone does after hearing that story. This, although the paper route manager never said it, was the first time I got fired...

Fast forward to the summer of 1994. I was 14. Selected to participate in the mayor's summer youth program, I worked for a prominent bank in downtown Buffalo. During my internship I frequently interacted with a female coworker. One day I asked her, "Can you come help me? C'mon over. I don't bite." First, at fourteen how am I supposed to know about sexual harassment? Second, I was so bored at work I hated that job. Third, I was 14! To be honest, though, making $5 an hour in that day and age was pretty impressive. Working a 40-hour work week, I was bound to have some major change. But sure enough, after two and a half days I was fired. Damn sexual harassment. Fired!

A year or so passed and I landed a job at the golden arches on Main and Utica, more popularly known as McDonald's...two all-beef patties, special sauce on a sesame seed bun. Yeah, you know the drill.

I started off in the grill section, which I quickly mastered. I was like Calvin in the old 90s commercial. I moved up, learning the register, runner window, and drive thru. Life was sweet. So sweet that I thought I could get over one night, as if I were not making enough money already and I had nothing better to spend my money on but food. I was leaving work and was ready to order my take-out. But instead of allowing the manager to ring up my order using my fifty percent discount like I should have, I got greedy. I told the person I worked with to stuff my food in the bag and I would say I only had one chicken sandwich and a drink. In reality I had a chicken sandwich meal, an upsized drink and an additional extra crispy chicken sandwich, both with lettuce, tomatoes, (an extra charge) and cheese. The manager sat back and watched as I put my food in a bag, told the cashier what I had, let him ring it up, and took my change. Not only was he watching, he told a co-worker to come to the back office and watch it with him on the cameras. He never alerted me to the fact that he was on to me. Never winked and sure enough did not even bother to ask twice if my order was correct.

Guess what happened next? A couple days later the store manager, Annie, called me in to say I was caught stealing. The difference between the meals was probably $3.00 and over $3.00 I was fired. They could have written me up, given me a warning or something. But I made the decision to steal. I made the decision to lie and cheat the system. I was already getting fifty percent off and could have even asked for the extra food. I learned that day it was not better to attempt to get over on those who are looking out for you. A lesson that came to bite me in the ass later with my own children doing the exact same things, trying to get over on me.

Fast forward a year and a half year to 1997. I graduated, the only black male in the top ten percent of my class. I was considered the leader of the school, class president, and recipient of several honors on Awards Day. I say "considered" because my junior year I ran against two other students for class president. Somehow the girl who won, Tia, beat me by one vote and the whole class president/vice president ordeal went south. What the teachers decided to do was form a leadership class later that fall and they placed me in it. Apparently, they saw my innate ability to lead and wanted me to do so. I ended up being a natural speaker during my senior year and erupting the crowd was one of my favorite things to do. Not only did I achieve that, but more importantly I became a proud Morehouse College freshman.

I did not have much money and got two credit cards as a freshman. The bills piled up. I was not taught how to manage a credit card, pay bills, or handle money, so I was balling with two $1,000 cards. I worked to at least pay the minimum, right? Sure, but I did not even know how to do that because the bill went to my granny's house in Buffalo, New York. I know I was a sad excuse back then, but you do not know what you just do not know. Parents, this is why it is imperative to teach your children about banking, credit, credit cards, interest rates, borrowing, and the negotiating power they have that they just do not know about.

So sure enough, I found a job working at the sneaker store in the famous Lenox Mall. I thought I had money lined up for me in my path…but it was kind of like the scene from the movie *Gladiator*, when Maximus is falsely accused, captured, and thrown into a pit, fighting for his freedom. I was a freshman enrolled full-time at the black Harvard for men. My assistant manager attended Morris Brown College, another school within the Atlanta university center. The reason that is important is because there are always rivalries among schools, but the one between Morehouse and Spelman Colleges versus Clark Atlanta University and Morris Brown College was epic. When I attended Morehouse and Spelman, the student body was told we were the cream of the crop, the tip of the top, better than the best! Thoughts, images, and stories of the heralded greatness issuing from our institutions suggested that anyone selected to be a part of this family could not only aspire to be great, but he could <u>be</u> great!

However, greatness eluded me. I will never forget the day that changed my life. That morning I called to see if I was on the schedule and if my money was in. While waiting to pick up my check, I was called to the store for an emergency. Unsure of what was going on, I made my way to the mall. When I arrived, management directed me to a small back office where an officer questioned me like I was a criminal. Not more than a month on the job, I was accused by the assistant manager of stealing some size fourteen Penny Hardaway sneakers. She alleged that I gave them to my friend, switching them out for his old shoes. At the time I did not understand the charges against me, so I thought she meant I took the shoes.

So first, I have worn a size nine or nine and a half for as long as I can remember. I think the biggest I have ever worn was a ten narrow. Anyway, I went to court, but she never showed up. My case was bound over to the state and I was put in a holding cell. After eight hours, I could not call anyone and missed out on my Valentine's Day date with my girlfriend, but nonetheless fired.

Had I listened to my mom back then I would probably be rich or at least had a lump sum of money and perhaps some residual payments from a settlement. My mother advised I countersue for defamation of character and who knows the possibilities? I could have won. At least I believe that now, but obviously that is ancient history... My reputation was impeccable back then, fresh out of high school with honors. But I chose not to listen to my mother at that young age for no other reason than I did not know what to do or how to go about initiating a lawsuit. Both actions were conscious decisions on my part.

Not long after that I landed a job with a local 100% black owned financial institution, Citizens Trust Bank in Atlanta, Georgia. They saw something in me too and wanted to promote me to branch manager. They even arranged a meeting with Mike Stuart, my current manager. As I sat in <u>his</u> office chair, they told me I could literally start from the bottom, the teller line, and work my way up to be the man. But while working a transaction for a customer who was in line, a gentleman jumped out of line and came over to what "looked to him" like an open window. He spoke, asking me to take his transaction. I ignored him at first because I did not want to mess up the current transaction. Then after waiting for a moment I acknowledged him. He wanted me to take his transaction right there. In "my young ass mind" he objected to standing in line like the other customers. So, I said, "Sir, this is not a teller window." And what do babies do when the pacifier goes pop on the floor? You guessed it! Kick and scream. He reported me to the CEO, James Young. Not long after that I was fired. I did not know that he was a shareholder for the bank and was supposed to get preferential treatment.

The next position was another teller job with First Union, which eventually became Wachovia. I liked Wachovia too. But I ran into trouble when I counted my money drawer way too fast and was out of balance more than 3 times in 3 different months. A discrepancy of more than five dollars was considered cause for dismissal. But I got canned for being ten dollars short at month's beginning and ten dollars over at month's end. Exactly 10 bucks! At the end of May 2002, I took a two-week vacation. Before I left, my drawer was $10 short. When I returned to work, I found that same ten dollars, but that did not matter. Still fired…May 30, 2002. Had I waited just two days

I could have kept my job and not suffered the humiliation of being fired yet again.

All I needed to do back then was not be out of balance more than once in a 90-day period. Here is the trick: in a bank they want you to work quickly and make no mistakes, but work efficiently so that everyone is moving along and there are no long wait times. Working quickly but also slowly enough not to make a mistake or make people wait is an illusion that I could never hold at that time.

That year was filled with joy as well as continued misfortune. In 2002, I got married and my wife and I had our first-born, Jeremiah. We were friendly with a young woman in our apartment complex who happened to be pregnant at the same time. She had just begun working for the Georgia

Department of Human Resources and suggested I apply for a position. After my initial application went through, I landed a position with the state. I actually enjoyed working there for the year, but once election time came around the governor cut the number of positions by nearly half. He informed employees that anyone could transfer to the county office or reapply for his/her current position if the position was still available. After conferring with my wife, we concluded that since we were in the process of purchasing a home, it would be ideal to live closer to both our jobs. Unfortunately, after eliminating so many positions, the governor brought in new staff to man his offices. After several attempts to advance, I finally accepted the fact that my efforts to secure a better position were futile.

I worked hard or so I thought. Like most people who goof off at work, I am positive I did my share of it, but not to my detriment and definitely not to the degree that it would necessitate my dismissal. However, I remember it clearly. When I returned from lunch one afternoon, the manager, Pat, came over to my cubicle, walked me down to the 2nd floor, and pink slipped me even though it was a white separation notice. Still got the slip. But she waited until 4:00 p.m. to do so. I was angry. By now you get the point - fired. This was December 2004.

Now let me shed some light on yet another firing, so you do not think I am just this bum on the corner or that I do not like to or want to work. About a year later almost to the day I took my next position, which was with Sprint/Nextel. Through no fault of my own, I was eventually laid off, but the manager promised to rehire me at another location; however, when the time came to reinstate me, she suggested I accept a severance package and continue to collect unemployment, which was about to run out just before my birthday. Boy, was I sick. No money on my birthday... agh! You cannot tell, but I screamed inside...right there...

In the meantime, I tried to cut grass and start a t-shirt company, both of which failed miserably. I just could not seem to secure landscaping contracts with residents in my neighborhood and no one wanted to buy the t-shirts I was selling. I ended up giving 95% of them away...

In fact, the last job (circa 2008) I had was as a debt collector for a company in Buffalo, New York.

One afternoon I was joking around with a female coworker, holding her arm to stop her from walking away. She did not like it and said so. I thought it was dropped then, but nope. I got a follow-up email from her. Then my manager and supervisor spoke to me. Finally, human resources got involved. No notice. No warning. You guessed it - fired. Before that I had been out of work for about 8 months or so... Lemme add them up for you guys... nope, it was 9 months from 5/14/07 until 2/25/08... long time to be without a job...

The next job I took was working for Home Depot. The Orange Box! I loved Home Depot, quickly making quite a few new friends. And this firing came just as easy. One would think the company would have fired me after my arrest... Oh wait.. yeah.. let me tell y'all about that dumb decision I made.

My then wife and I had made plans to travel to Buffalo, New York to visit my family for the weekend. We rented a van and prepped to go. I, being the "super smart guy", looked at the schedule which was printed 2 weeks prior and noticed a two-hour gap in the schedule where there was no coverage. I came up with a brilliant plan to tell my supervisor about the lapse and suggest, as any stellar employee would, that I'd leave before the break to handle a few things and then return in time to make sure we had coverage.

En route to the store after my break, I got off at my normal exit and smashed into the back of a woman's car. Knowing my license was recently suspended, I decided not to flee the scene, as my plan for that weekend was to pay the fine and reinstate my license prior to returning to Atlanta from the weekend festivities. Of course, I got a ticket and was arrested in front of my children for driving on a suspended license. My former wife was crying; however, I told her to call our police officer friend for instructions as to what to do to get me out of jail. I called the store and advised them I would not be returning because I was temporarily unable to cover my shift... i.e. arrested! But that did not get me fired!! Noooooooooooooo. What did then?

One afternoon I was driving a forklift while my flagger walked in front of the vehicle to warn customers that we were coming. I should interject that he was a brand spanking new employee. And guess who trained him? You got it - ME!!! While driving the forklift the metal corner of a table saw hooked onto the forklift and snapped off. No damage anywhere. No incident. No one was hurt. No one was close to the incident. However, employees are required to report every incident that takes place inside the store. Seeing that nothing was broken and no damage was done I kept moving. But you know what I am about to tell you.

Of course the new guy follows every single rule to the letter of the law. I however looked at what happened similar to dropping a bag of quick concrete. Nothing happened, pick it up and keep moving. So, a few hours later my supervisor brought me into the office and asked why I did not report the incident. That's right. Fired again! By this time, I hated these words, "We are gonna have to let you go." Or, "Your services are no longer needed." Or whatever phrasing is used.

The next job I picked up was working for another collection agency in Atlanta, where I was employed for over 2 years. Unbeknownst to me, the company planned to offer me a promotion. Before this materialized, I requested a transfer to another department. What I should have done is just taken a few days off and enjoyed Christmas and my birthday with my family. Once I returned in January, I would have been a salaried employee with a collections team of about 10 to 15 to coach. And I would have been making the same money if not more than the department to which I asked to be transferred. I honestly was tired of getting a lower pay and my impatience led me to what I am about to discuss.

So, to make a long story short, I was fired on what I believe to be a technicality. Certain states have strict laws that require debt collection agencies to provide specific information during phone calls to a person in debt. At the time I was the number two collector in the building. Floor managers regularly reviewed collectors' calls, so when my manager examined my calls for that month, she found an error. I think it was not a coincidence that she was looking at me with a narrow focus. I believe it was because I was gaining momentum and becoming one of the best. The company already had a crew of elite collectors and here was this new, arrogant, top-notch collector coming for what they seemed to hold dear - coveted accounts that were only distributed to those who were the best. Their crew had been together for

2 to 3 years prior to my arrival and I was definitely the outsider. I fought for each of my accounts I collected and, in my opinion, I was not going to just lay down easy if someone attempted to take from me. Everyone had his or her own opinion of the situation, but I was walked out of the building midday. Fired. Again.

After collections, I landed a job with Alpine Access, working there part-time for less than 5 months. After Alpine, I went to Convergys, both work from home companies. This started to put stress on my family life because I worked at night. Also, my former wife was not ready to handle the pressure of working full time and being a full time single married mom. I was home. I cooked. But I was not able to be present because I had to work in the garage or bedroom or wherever it was quiet enough to take calls. As time went on, I left the company because I found I could work from home for myself making the same money I was already making and not have a stressed-out spouse. So, I fired myself.

Let me say this, "You will never be able to replace time lost away from your family." No matter how many deals you miss out on, you will and can find others that are better are equal to what you lost. No matter how much money you make or lose, it can be replaced. Do not sacrifice even one minute of time away from family because TIME is the only thing you will not get more of once it is gone. You may have another day, but if it is still filled with things that take priority over family, then you will never get back those precious moments. I had to learn this hard lesson and while it eventually was the right decision, it was not one that I made lightly or with rushed judgement. Consider your options. Find time for those who care about you the most and go out and execute like a boss! You can. Just decide to do it and go after it.

Let me say this, you will never be able to replace time lost away from your family.

R. J. Torrence, I

All of these job losses taught me a lesson. I needed to change my viewpoint on how I worked. It was part arrogance in the early days that got me fired, part ignorance in other instances. In some cases, I just did not give too many cares. I needed to work to earn a living, but I also needed to figure out what worked best for me and how I could make an honest living. In time, I learned what to do about work and the best choice came from working for myself. I had not yet learned how to humble myself enough to constantly submit to overbearing authority. To be very honest I did not want to do it either. I felt I was better than those who were in that position. What I now know is that they were there for a reason and it was not up to me to try to oust them from their thrones, but to become better as a person and learn how to handle life and people. To learn not to wish for fewer problems but to acquire more skill. To learn not to wish for things to get easier, but to become better at my job. I was king of blaming everyone else for why I was not successful. It was comfortable.

What I had to do was embark on a journey of self-improvement, a plan of self-enrichment. I read more books, focused more on accomplishing the tasks that I knew would carry me forward. I tried harder to be better in every way. I learned not to give up. What I hated most was knowing that I was the reason for the problems I faced. Like so many of you, I attracted these issues because of the person I was. If you become a better person then you will see your problems and issues change too. It is quintessential for you to become better today than you were yesterday. Take 90 days and begin something new.

In the next few pages write down behaviors and habits you have created that you know you should stop. Then write down things you should stop saying. Then list self-sabotaging actions and thoughts that you know do not lead to the place where you want to be.

Finally, ask yourself this question, "Why? Why do I keep doing these things?" Without blaming your mom, dad, anyone else, history, past failures, or what you did not get or should've gotten. Figure out why you do what you do. Then determine what you can immediately do to stop the cycle.

"Don't wish it was easier wish you were better. Do not wish for less problems wish for more skills. Don't wish for less challenge wish for more wisdom." Jim Rohn

HOW I CREATED THE GAME

In 2006, my then wife and I were introduced to network marketing by our friends Watson and Joyce. She found that the business was a great way to create additional income and got started right away. Like most folks who begin a network marketing or multilevel marketing business, she created a list and started calling all of her warm market which included family and friends to garner support. I, who fell asleep during the presentation in my man chair, was hardly interested, even though I had been introduced to the same company during my college years.

She struggled. I mean really struggled. No one answered the phone or came to an appointment or even wanted to listen. She did three-way calls and all the right things one should do when beginning the business. I am sure many of you can relate to being called by a friend or family member saying, "I want to share my new business with you." I watched as she struggled and did not really care either. It wasn't so much that I was nonchalant about her frustration; it was more a lack of empathy on my part. She wanted it to work. She wanted to do it her way. It was her business so I stayed out of the way for as long as I could. The company had an enticing promotion; if we sold/marketed the right amount of pre-paid legal family plans and had the right number of new business partners within a certain time frame, then we'd position ourselves to be very close to the top of the compensation plan.

One day when she was not working, I decided to talk to the guy who brought us into the business and ask what we needed to do to reach the level of success they desired. Of course, I told her to sit back and watch me work. I, being more business savvy, knew exactly what to do to get the needed business partners to advance in the company. So we advanced. I did what was needed to move us forward and I believe that is the moment when the resentment set in. I achieved in less than ten days what she could not do in thirty days and thus created dissension. However, it was a good thing for me to step in, or so I thought, because indirectly it led to my board game design story.

Fast-forward two years into the business. Just when I was being heralded as a new, exciting, upcoming leader, things started to fail. First my marriage, then the house we had purchased a couple years prior, and then our business. We moved from our home and found a temporary place not far from where we were. We struggled even in the new place. Amidst the struggle, we had a real heart-to-heart, talking about how and why we failed in the business and why others were not succeeding either.

As I lay on the floor in the living room, I distinctly remember hearing Jim Rohn's voice on YouTube, 'Building Your Network Marketing Business'. It played in my head, saying, "Do not ask why. It is the way it is." He encouraged listeners not to ask why because doing so would drive you up a wall. Suddenly, it hit me like a ton of bricks. People fail because they have not learned how to succeed. I recalled that the release of Robert Kiyosaki's book, *Rich Dad, Poor Dad* and his board game *Cash Flow 101*, started a revolution in the real estate and investing arena. He showed and talked about how to create payoff liabilities by building up your assets. His books taught many how to buy investment properties. And his board game taught patience in the process of buying and selling real estate and stock investments.

I concluded if he could do it, so could I. Not that I had the same fame or notoriety, but I could still design a game to help people. That was the point at which I told my wife I was going to create a network marketing board game to teach others how to build their business. And I think for the first time I could remember, she believed in me and said, "Go for it!"

It was July 17, 2007 when it all began. I pulled out a huge piece of construction paper and drew the layout. I made every card I could think of. I wrote out rules and tips on how to win. I designed the money for the game. My mind was exploding with ingenuity. Watching it come along, I had even more incentive to keep going. Later that week at Stonecrest Panera Bread, I ran into Joseph Washington, author of the *Breaking the Spirit of Average.* I explained to him that I would be creating a multi-level marketing board game. He simply commented, "If you do not finish the game in two years, I will do it myself." That lit a blazing fire under me. While I had no clue of how to create a board game, I figured somehow I could do it and make it appear out of thin air. I was not going to leave it to chance, but allowed for a little luck and good planning to take place. It was only when I fully committed to seizing this great opportunity that things begin to align. I needed a name for the game. Originally it was going to be called *FIRE YOUR BOSS*, because most who preach the sermon of networking marketing talk about the joys of the money made and the freedom of being able to walk away from their conventional income after building a sustainable business. I hated that name and played with *You're Fired*, but at the time there was a reality television show on which would-be entrepreneurs who did not make the cut were fired. I definitely did not want to be associated with that show or the celebrity personality hosting it. I called John, my buddy and fellow business partner in Florida, and he was super excited too. I finally settled on *FIRED, the network marketing board game.* Why? Because I thought it was clever and I liked the idea of being clever and having something everyone could easily remember. A name that would stick with people long after I walked away from them, even if they did not recall my name or what I said. The company would be called PNKSLP LLC (pink slip). Why? Because when you are FIRED, you get a PNKSLP!!! That was clever. It caught on with anyone I told, but I did not tell everyone. Just a few.

We moved a couple times after that, but I still continued to work on plans for the game. My first design was a hideous pink and brown board with a pastel blue background. Just imagine how disgusting that would have been, but I lived through it. (Trust me it is okay to laugh out loud with me). I needed a logo for the money and the denominations and created both on Microsoft word. It was coming together, but it was not a reality yet. At the time, I started playing flag football with a few guys I had met. One Sunday I told the guys about the game and explained I needed to design it. They introduced me to Brian who was a recent college graduate and his jam was graphic design. BOOM! It was a match made in heaven or so I thought.

I hated the first color copy he made, but he helped me a lot and yes, I paid him. It wasn't much and his design was too edgy and overly sophisticated, so I was not thrilled with the work, but I kept letting him try his hand. I got the playing cards made and that was a huge part of the success. While I designed them front and back, I could not make them in the format needed for printing.

In the midst of Brian helping me, I told my mentor Dewong Lucas, author of *Fighting the Bear,* about my game. He was a man I trusted not to steal my work or my idea. Although I was secretly scared, I confided in him anyway. He loved the idea and gave me the best help I have ever had. I told him I hated the design of the game and he asked me to send it to him. Previously, I sent a non-disclosure agreement to anyone who looked at the project or worked with me or with whom I shared the idea. I had to protect my work, vision, and ideas. I sent it to Dewong, but what he did before that changed my life. He said to go into any store where games are sold and look at the most popular games. I was to find their dominant colors in order to help me figure out what my game should look like. When I shared the results of my research with him, he promised to get back to me on January 7, 2008. Like a kid waiting to open Christmas presents, I waited. When the day finally arrived, I was working at Home Depot. I waited all day for my phone to ring, but there was no call. When I got off work, I phoned him, having heard many, many times that the fortune is in the follow up, meaning if you do not follow up with someone about your idea you could possibly miss out on the fortune.

Dewong said he had not forgotten and that he would reach out to me soon. I had no idea what he was planning, but I just knew he was going to help me in some way. And then, January 8, 2009 it happened! I received an email and I immediately screamed out loud, scaring my co-worker Damaris. I cried because what he sent was an excellent prototype of exactly what I needed. Perfect color scheme. Perfect layout. Imperfect spelling, but after all, he had worked until 3:00 a.m. to finish it and send it to me. He was a man of his word! He helped! Of course, my other graphic artist was super jealous and hated the new design. He did not want to work with it, but since I was the creator and I knew what I saw spoke to my inner self, I did not allow his misguided mind to deter me from what I knew was the perfect design for MY project.

Mr. Lucas, as I called him back then, was on the money! He told me to play the game over and over until I knew everything that could happen. I wanted so bad to print the game, but looked everywhere and could not find a place online. On a random evening at Kinko's (before it became FedEx Kinko's™) I was asking a clerk about her printing ability and she explained that she could print my game as long as it was in PDF format. Little did she know it was in a protected PDF file, so I was a little closer to the realization of my dream. I then looked on the web for places to manufacture the game or at least print one copy. Through my research I found an awesome company that would print 500, but it was pricey. While disheartened, I did not leave their site empty handed. On the same site I found a board game jr. kit which included everything I needed to make my own copy as long as I could mount it on the blank 10" x 10" they provided. They even gave instructions on how to mount it. I was thrilled and all I needed was to figure out how to copyright or patent it.

Mr. Lucas again, chimed in with timely wisdom saying, "You could spend a whole lot of money trying to patent it and fail to put money into making your vision come true. Search the web, look for network marketing board games and if you do not find anything like yours, then you will be spinning your wheels attempting to do what may or may not need to be done."

It was only when I fully committed to seizing this great opportunity that things began to align.

I did not know back in 2008 that it was not time for the game to come out, so I just kept going, kept doing the trials, kept practicing the game, fine-tuning the cards. I played the game in real time and in my head over and over and over again. I remember wanting my hometown friends and family to support me, so I took the board game to Buffalo, New York, hoping for an enthusiastic reception. Even though I invited at least 40 to 50 people, only 2 showed up. I learned that not everyone will come out to celebrate your new venture before you actually achieve success.

I remember a test game night here in Lithonia, Georgia where 13 friends showed up. I had my kids cutting out the cards, gluing them together, making my own money sheets. My best friend could not even show up because he had to take his son to the Georgia Dome to be in a football game. Still, I got great feedback from people about what the game should look like, how it should flow, how it should work. And I probably had 250 to 300 cards among all 4 decks. One of the testers suggested I needed a ratio of 3:1 or 4:1, referring to the ratio of good cards to bad cards. That completely changed the game.

That was back in 2010, when I was still trying to get a manufacturer. I thought I needed $20k to produce the game based on the site I mentioned earlier. They would produce and ship 500 copies for that amount. I did not know then what I know now. That next year, after not launching the game, I entered into the Shark Tank competition on 4/13/13. I knew then I was ready and this was my time. I was going to make this dream a success.

I got a room across from the Fox Theatre in downtown Atlanta and prepared my suit so I could look impressive and wow the producers with my awesome concept, but that did not happen. I was number thirty-one in line and figured that today was destiny because my birthday was on the 31st and the stars could not align more perfectly or at least in my head. I did not realize that Shark Tank wants you to sell them a story... I just had a great idea. A great product with great margins that solves the problem of what network marketing is for the tactile/kinesthetic learner. I met plenty of people standing in the line as well as staying in the hotel across the street from the auditions. I ended up meeting a lady named Trisha who designed a Christian board game and her manufacturer was in China. I could get 1,000 copies of my game from them for the same price I had been quoted by the company on the internet. But I still needed to raise 15k to 20k to produce and launch *FIRED*. Previously I had met with 3 investors, but I just could not get the money.

I met the first prospective investor while having a lunch date with my ex. Afterwards I called him day in and day out to schedule an appointment. Although I did not want to annoy him, I continuously followed up to make sure I was in the forefront of his mind. I wanted 15k for 15% equity... a huge risk to take on such an unknown, but I knew it would sell. I had watched so many people play the game, always experiencing that ah-ha moment at some point. For me, this meant that if <u>they</u> got it, others would too. The first investor I met with was in the steel business and he only wanted to invest in my company if I was turning it into an app. And since tech was his thing, he declined to invest. I was devastated because it took me 30 minutes to find his office and 3 to 4 months for him to actually sit down and look at the prototype of the game. I think my major mistake was not having him play the game. Everyone who plays it loves it. He needed a better understanding of what it was. Just describing it and allowing him to see the game wasn't convincing enough. Had he experienced that ah-ha moment while playing the game, my belief is that he would have jumped right on board.

My next step was to try Kickstarter, a crowd funding platform, but I failed, raising only $720. On this platform if you do not raise the exact amount, you get 0% of the funds raised. Per Kickstarter's instructions, I made the video, filled in all the blanks, and expected my friends and family to spread the word. No one did anything. I had a couple shares from my mom and a few more shares from my brothers because I begged them. And that was that. I was so demoralized that I thought nobody believed in me. I wanted to quit. And for many days, weeks, and months that is exactly what I did. However, every time someone asked me what I did, I explained that I designed a game.

The enthusiasm of a few friends and family got me back at it again. It just took a few people to believe in me to reignite my fire and sometimes that spark is all we need. The only thing I wanted was to publish the game, make some money to feed my family, and help others by making it possible for them to play the game. For 20+ years of my life, all I did was get fired! I was at a low point, a point where I stopped believing in myself if no one else believed in me.

The enthusiasm of a few friends and family got me back at it again. It just took a few people to believe in me to reignite my fire and sometimes that spark is all we need.

I did not quit though. I tried again. In December 2012, I logged on to IndieGoGo, an alternate crowdfunding site. I stuck with it through February 2013 and this time I was a little more successful. When all was said and done, I raised $2,050. Although it was not the 15k I had hoped for, I still needed every penny of it. The sad fact is that I had close friends who did not contribute a dime toward the project and even though they helped by sharing the site after I pleaded with them, their lack of financial backing made me sad. To be honest, I believe I launched the project at the wrong time. It ran from Christmastime through Valentine's Day. A major lesson learned was that people will buy what they want when they want and support when they have extra.

I begged my ex to send messages to her friends to back the project by donating $20. She refused and as the days passed, we argued about her support. The more I begged and pleaded with her to reach out to her friends, the more defiant she became. I felt the world closing in on me and my failures piling up. Again and again. This hurt me to my core. I kept getting fired and finally found something to help me break this pattern, but the person who mattered most, the one who would benefit from it, refused to help. I finally gave up asking and started asking her friends myself. This was an even worse idea that blew up in my face. A bitter argument ensued. My idea of how to proceed with the project, doing it my way, was not the way she wanted to help. I think that after ninety-five percent of the project was complete, she may have asked a couple of friends to contribute and I literally mean a couple of friends.

I think that the seeds of doubt, bitterness, and resentment set in way back in 2006. Remember when I explained that I "showed her up" and improved our ranking in the business she started? I think that never died and only built a deeper resentment and disdain for me and my ideas.

Here was my math. The goal was to raise $20,000. We each had about 3,000 friends on our social media pages. We shared or had in common approximately 300 mutual friends of the 3,000. So give or take 2,700 friends between the two of us. Many of these people knew us well enough visit our website and friend us. My thought was to get at least

1,500 of these friends to contribute $20 to my project, enabling me to easily reach my goal.

Clearly that did not happen. What did happen was magical. It was the appointed time for the right things to happen and all the stars aligned at the exact same time.

I went through all of 2014 without making a single copy of the game. In December of 2014, I joined a board game group on the immensely popular social media site Facebook. One day I asked another member if he knew of a manufacturer who would produce fewer than 500 copies of my game or who charged less than 15k. He replied almost immediately with information on a website where I could produce them one at time or reduce the price by ordering in bulk, starting with only 25 copies of the game.

During this time, I was an executive member of a local Chamber of Commerce. At one of our meetings I was introduced to Lisa and Ursula. They loved how passionate I was about the game and both wanted to invest. I talked margins with each of them and promised a return. Both wanted to be silent investors because they believed in me and THIS shot my confidence through the roof. I did not care that my ex was not supportive then. I figured I had to go it alone. And alone I went. Two investors. I had gone from no or minimal support to believers!

I had not achieved yet. I just had to finish the last bit of graphic design work and then I could start selling them. I still needed to play the game more, but I also needed to get copies to sell. Once I discovered the website, I could have started with the buy and sell or sell and buy. In other words, I could buy the copies then sell off the inventory. Or knock on each door one by one, close the sale, order the game, and ship it out. I hired one last graphic designer, Gene, in 2014. He fine-tuned the cards to the liking of the manufacturer's specifics and off I went. I spoke with Lisa to set up the date to invest, uploaded everything to the site for the initial purchase, entered her credit card information, and voila! A few short weeks later the mail lady came by with 5 boxes. Fifty copies of my dream come true! Now the real work began. This should have been a joyous time for me, but my failing marriage hung over my head.

WHY A FAILED MARRIAGE?

How does all this tie in one may ask? Why share your private business? Honestly, I am not going to tell you every detail. But part of *The Edge of Greatness* is rooted in the decisions you make. Deciding to marry without the right amount of information will lead to disaster. Also when I do share, I hope to help someone else avoid the disasters I faced.

My marriage was doomed from the beginning. Why? How do I know that? At the time I did not. I was young and stupid. I thought I knew everything and that if I found a woman, I could make her a wife.

In the words of my friend Lakia Brandenburg, the #1 wife coach in the business and author of *Picture Perfect,* "All married women are not wives!" That goes without saying, but the reverse is true for married men; all married men are not husbands. My marriage was doomed because I did not take the time to get to know myself and what I needed before bringing someone else into my dysfunction. I did not know what kind of woman I wanted to marry. I ignored the red flags that were flapping in the wind from the very beginning. Doing so caused our relationship to deteriorate. What you ignore will be the cause of your breakup.

Amidst the arguing, her spitting in my face, me leaving twice while she was pregnant, cursing, rejection, lack of support, screaming, bitterness, anger, resentment, and verbal abuse, we tried several counselling sessions to mend what was broken. We were both toxic and unwilling to love or change. On the outside we came and went and seemed fine, but there was no public display of affection when we were at "war". Literally no "f's" were given. Yes, there were times when we were on good terms, but the exacerbation of the bad seemingly nullified the good things.

The last straw was the initial 90-day separation, which was supposed to be a break. But we devised a divorce plan if the separation did not work and that ultimately led to divorce. This may sound like your story. Your marriage may be failing. I am in no position to tell <u>you</u> what to do. That is between you and your spouse. I will say, "Do NOT stay in an abusive relationship hoping one day he or she (yes, women are abusers too) will get better. Maybe you are the hurtful one and need to step away. Do what you need to for yourself and heal. See a therapist! It is not that bad. I pinky promise. They will help you if you practice the things you discover on a daily basis and put in the work to become better. Do not just marry because your prospective spouse looks good on paper or the two of you look great in pictures. Optics will hurt you. Just because it looks good does not mean it actually is good.

Base your relationship on trust, great communication, compromise, satisfying your core needs, compassion and growth. I am sure there are a ton of other things too, but that is a great start. I wanted to tell you how I failed so I can tell you how

I attracted a better person because I became a better, whole, and healed person. And so can you.

Ten signs I ignored which contributed to the deterioration of my first marriage:

1) I stopped caring because I was rejected in the 1st few months.
2) I married the person I thought she could be, not who she currently was.
3) I craved power and authority when as the head of the family I already had it.
4) I sought to dominate her rather than love her.
5) I stopped flirting.
6) I no longer loved first, hard, or selflessly.
7) I left twice, both times while she was pregnant.

8) I neglected to be the giver and leader.

9) I stopped being compassionate.

10) I did not practice becoming a better person and failed to realize I needed a therapist to change or relearn who I was. I was lost as an individual and hurting. I did not heal properly.

10 Things I Did to Have a Better Mate

1) I became a whole person.
2) I enjoyed being alone as well as having the companionship of others
3) I took time after my divorce WAS FINALIZED to heal before getting into a relationship.

4) I took myself on dates to rediscover what I liked and loved.

5) I practiced loving myself so I could give to someone else.

6) I practiced being a good mate even though I was not in a relationship, so that when the relationship came along it no longer became a practice. The learned behavior became automatic.

7) I became the person someone I wanted to be with would want to be with.

8) I listened to others for solid relationship advice.

9) I apologized to those whom I did wrong and hurt because of my prior arrogance.

10) I found someone who loved me the way I wanted to be loved and was willing to compromise on SOME things because I was not perfect and neither was she.

GIVE YOURSELF TIME TO HEAL

The first 12 months after divorce I focused on recovery.

The second 12 months after divorce I focused on rebuilding.

The third 12 months after divorce I focused on reestablishing myself.

WHERE IS THE EDGE OF GREATNESS?

First, before I get into all of that, thank you. Yes, you. For reading. I am honored that you purchased, read, and listened to my book. Second, I pray it blesses you and helps guide you to the source of your own power. I hope that when you are presented with an opportunity and must make a choice, you choose wisely!

Lastly, for me, without God, I would fail. So ask for God's help. My entire book is about what you can do for you. Every day you get to take part in the miracle, the process of your life.

Now--

The edge of greatness is found at the intersection of opportunity and choice. When you are faced with both you must decide. Remember that not deciding is still a decision. Avoidance is not necessarily the best choice because at that point you allow others to decide. YOU. MUST. DECIDE. Making a choice puts you in the driver's seat. How to make a choice? Think it through. Wait. Seek help from those wiser than you. Then make a decision based on whatever you think is best for you. Be sure that you are not putting others in harm's way, injuring others, or causing harm to yourself.

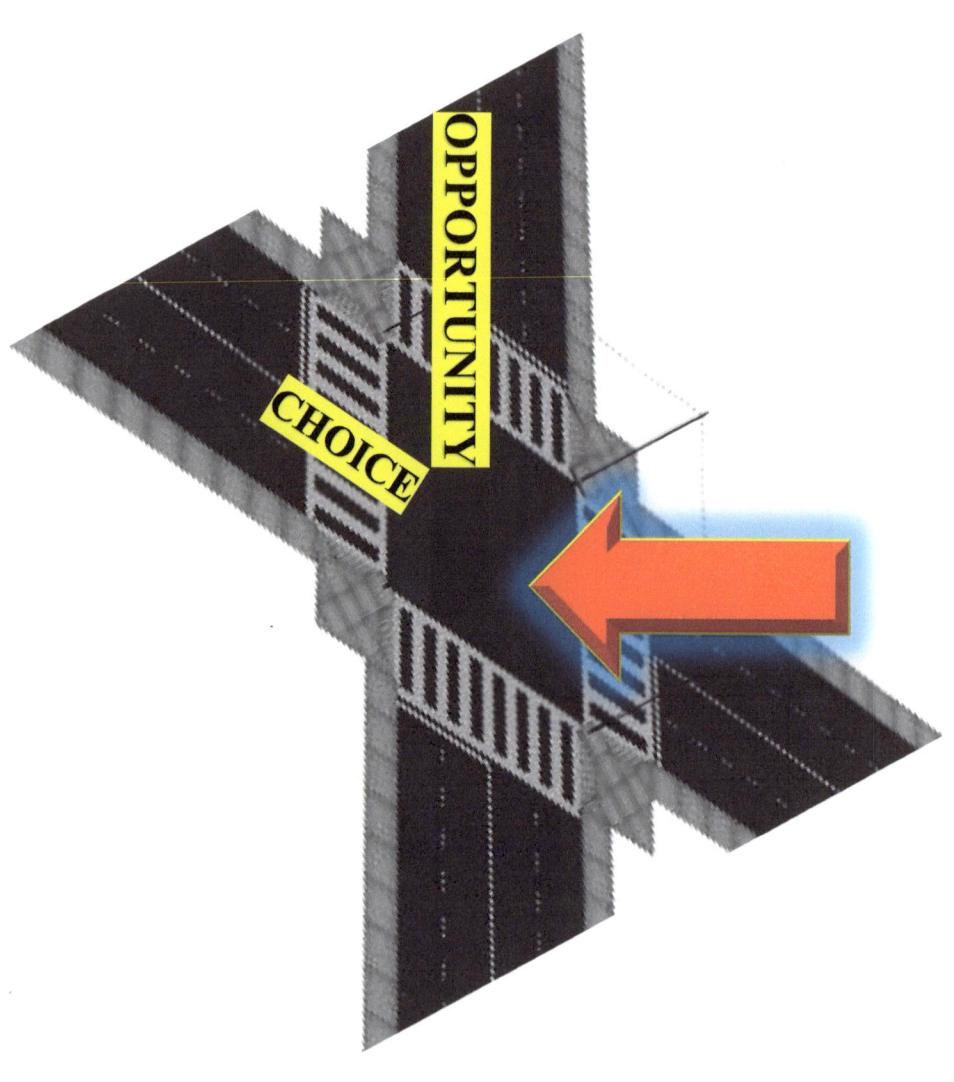

Let's look at the word OPPORTUNITY. If broken down and flipped a bit, you will see two base words *oppo-* and *unity*. Most often success comes when OPPO-sition meets UNITY… coming together or being united, joined as a whole. Opposition is defined as resistance or dissent expressed in action or argument.

People miss opportunity/greatness because it is dressed in overalls and looks like work. Most opportunity comes from a truth that is revealed to you. You may identify a problem and come up with a solution. Other times it comes from making things slightly better. Ever look at a cellphone from year to year? The previous "new" model is only slightly better than the last. The camera might be better or have greater quality. An upgraded speak to text feature may be a modest improvement on last year's version.

Usually we fail to grasp a new opportunity because we are met with resistance and what I have found, which may work for you, is to attack the resistance with actionable steps to overcome whatever is stopping you. For example, you want to be married but are not in a relationship. "How do I get there, you ask?" Finding a mate is not the first step because there are people everywhere. The first step is to decide what kind of person you need. Then filter all of the choices in front of you within the parameters of the person you need. Second, reevaluate your desires and make sure they are not superficial or too picky. Then to simplify it and get to the place of finding a healthy relationship, become the type of person the person you are looking for would like to date.

Be honest with yourself. Learn how to become self-aware and then practice the everyday behavior you want to exhibit once that person comes along. Then those habits will no longer be a conscious effort. More simply put, you will automatically act that way because you have been doing it for so long. You must consistently practice being who you want to become so that this becomes a part of who you are, not just something you do. Practice so that when the moment comes to actually do the thing you have been practicing, it is natural not forced.

You can substitute the word "marriage" in the above example or get a job, a college degree, forgiveness, healing, or even a clean home.

Remember the aim is not to harm others or do yourself harm. Other than that, go for what you know! It will take a little work daily, but it does not have to take forever.

You must consistently practice who you want to become so that this becomes a part of who you are, not just something you do. Practice so that when the moment comes to actually do the thing you have been practicing, it is natural not forced.

A FEW TIPS

You're never too old or young to embrace opportunity.

Every opportunity you have is accompanied by a crisis.

The average person limits himself or herself by hearing only the basic instructions.

To excel you must exceed average.

There are no shortcuts to greatness.

It takes fifteen years to become an overnight success.

Comments that follow the words you speak are supposed to validate what was said.

There are people who come into your life to help you and you should accept the help.

CONCLUSION

How does all this tie together?

When I was a child, I learned to make my own money by selling newspapers but under the guise of someone paying me what they thought I was worth -- thirty-five dollars weekly.

Then by sixteen, I figured I could be slick and get over by outsmarting a camera and a manager who was watching like a hawk. Twenty years later, at the age of thirty-six, I have learned that being slick got me nowhere! I was earning a decent wage, but I still continued down the path of getting fired religiously. It seemed to occur almost every two years. And nothing in my life felt worse than being relieved of my duties at work.

Fast forward to working in my late twenties and early thirties. I learned that I needed to take time to sit down and be still. I needed to stop thinking I was better than everyone and could outsmart everyone because my mind worked overtime. I could figure out how to solve everyone else's problems except the problem of me getting continuously fired!

I was a screwed up mess. I began to have a love/hate relationship with myself. I loved that I was smart enough to figure out how to create income but not smart enough to actually keep a job long enough to make that second income work and build. After all of the firings and learning to build income, I came up with the novel idea to create a board game and call it

FIRED! Why? Because that was the biggest part of my life's lessons. And because it so uniquely tied into what network marketing can become. A tool to FIRE your boss. My board game teaches people the business of network marketing while having fun at the same time.

At first, I did not learn anything from the firings. But in later years I learned that I needed to figure myself out. Figure out that what worked best for me and how I worked best. The board game, should you buy it, will help you or someone else. Play it. Buy it. Please.

This book was really my therapy after I lost everything. People turned their backs on me because of a half story told to them. But in the end love prevailed. I do not hate the people who left. I learned to be better and have more compassion.

I only really wanted to write about how I designed a board game and then it turned into so much more. I truly hope I have helped you. I hope that something I have said in these pages will change something for you, if not now, maybe in the future.

Let me tie the whole thing together for you. In a nutshell – I found a way to become un-fireable. Write a book. Publish a board game. Sell both. You cannot fire me from that! So take that, life! You gave me lemons. I planted an orchard, grew lemons, made lemonade, sold some lemons to the local farmers' markets. And I ain't quitting yet! Even after being kicked down what seemed like a gazillion times. I hope that you can take a page from me and let my life lessons teach you what not to do as well as what you, we, can do better.

Thank you. No, for real. Thank you. (Read that last line again, but much slower).

www.ingramcontent.com/pod-product-compliance
Lightning Source LLC
Chambersburg PA
CBHW041615220426
43670CB00004B/59